CARAMEL ONIONS

WRITTEN
BY FAATIMAH ABDUR-RAB

COVER DESIGN & ARTWORK
BY LABHALI RAZI

www.innerworldentertainment.com

Published: 2011

Printed and manufactured in the United States of America.

Editor, artwork and cover design by LaBhali Razi

ISBN: **987-0615579184**

www.innerworldentertainment.com

DEDICATION

I would like to dedicate my first book to my husband LaBhali, my children Jameela, Sullaiman, Jamar, Sayyid, Ishmael and my grand children Rayah and Kamaal. This is my family, my family that has been with me through everything. They have given me the inspiration to write this book as well as others. They've been with me through the happy times and the struggles, through the smiles and the tears. I dedicate this book to you because without your love and support I wouldn't have been able to write and complete it. Thank You and I Love You Very, Very Much.

CARAMEL ONIONS

www.innerworldentertainment.com

CONTENTS

	Web sites	i
1	Beginning My Adult Life	3
2	God Is Real	29
3	If I Only Knew	43
4	The Let Down	51
5	Dreaming	56
6	There Is Beauty In The Midst Of the Storm	65
7	My Life	78
8	My Love	86
9	Beware	90
10	Change Is Good	93

CARAMEL ONIONS

WEB SITES

http://www.innerworldentertainment.com/faatimah
http://www.showcasespot.com/profile/faatimahabdurrab

i

CARAMEL ONIONS

CHAPTER 1

Beginning My Adult Life

Talking about the beginning of my adult life is like talking about a rollercoaster ride. Everything in life is all over the place including your emotions because everything going on in the world. Life can be very stressful, it's survival of the fittest and if you don't take the time, stop, think and do your checklist for life you'll never know where you're going. (So choose your priorities wisely.)

ROLLER COASTER

I'm tired of going around on this roller coaster,

It's time to stop and try another ride.

A ride that is straight,

So I can go down that pathway.

I need to go down the right path,

So move out of my way, so that I can get pass.

It's time to move on to better things,

Cause heartache and pain is all this brings.

What do you want us to sweat and bleed?

Trying to get the things we need.

I know it's not easy and sometimes it's hard.

What do we need some kind of credit card,

To prove that were able and our credit is good.

We only have to prove ourselves to god above.

Everyone has hard times in life,

No one is perfect or without strife.

But why is it that I can't get by.

Why do I keep coming back here?

I don't know how many times or years.

I should have moved on to a higher place by now,

I work hard enough I don't see how.

I haven't went to a higher level or a different test,

Maybe it's because I've failed so I can't try the rest.

But all I know is that I do my best,

Trying to past the test called life.

AAHHH!!!!!

Disappointment is a horrible thing,

You can't think, you can't sing.

You just don't know what life brings.

What the hell is going on?

Things that seem right, is always wrong.

What do I do?

What can I do?

Should I live? Should I die?

Should I try to survive?

Or maybe I should just sit here and cry.

But Why?

Why do I try? Why do I try?

AAHHH!!!

WAKE UP

Race, Religion, Social Status,

Reasons for discrimination.

It's going on everywhere among us,

No one is immune, it happens to everyone.

When will it stop?

When will it end?

It doesn't matter if you're a cop

Or a civilian.

Rich, poor or middle class,

In the present and the past.

Every city, state, county and country

All around the world.

North, South, East, West

Even with little boys and girls.

It's in our home and in our schools

What must we do?

T T

T and T, what does it mean?

Terrorists and Tyrants is who it be.

What is the difference between the two?

There is no difference for me and you.

They are the same, they're both Murderers,

Except one is the oppressed and the other is the oppressor.

Just in case you don't know,

The oppressor is the bully,

The oppressed is being bullied,

Trying to protect his belongings.

What do you do when you're in the middle?

Your words aren't heard, you don't exist.

Trying to say please stop,

Can we bring this to an end?

It's not worth all the pain,

Of which it's only the beginning.

Stop hurting one another T and T,

Try to Love each other and let it be.

The wars you're having don't have to be.

WAR

War, what is it about?

Going to another country getting taken out.

With guns, mines, explosives and all,

While politicians sit home and watch you take the fall.

Fighting other countries on their behalf,

It's all about wealth and what they have.

They act like their trying to give you a hand,

When all they want is to take your land.

War, what is it about?

They'll only take you out.

War, they're getting paid,

On all the graves they've made.

War.

They act like they want to help you,

So they bring you to this place.

When all they think about is controlling you,

And how much money they'll make.

They don't care about you,

Or what you need.

They only want to own you,

They won't let you succeed.

To join the Army, Marines or the Navy,

Takes a person who's stupid or either crazy.

You'll never advance or get anywhere,

You'll only get death, heartache and despair.

That's War.

FED UP

Wanna be gangsters, dope dealers and thugs,

The shits about to start and that's on all my love.

We're fed up with the bullshit never took a hit,

The bud is alright don't mess with no glass stick.

The tension is rising, hates in the air,

Niggas getting killed blamed for a stare.

Murders on the rise, dope dealers getting paid,

The police are laughing; the man is still a slave.

When I wake up in the morning, I say to myself,

All praise is due to God for my health.

For allowing me to see another day,

Somehow a lot of people just don't feel that way.

Fed up with the bullshit.

Life can be dark with all the drugs and hate,

All you ever think about is just wanting to escape.

Tried to go to school never had no help,

Parents slaved for thirteen years never got no wealth.

Drugs in the community and aids on the rise.

Politicians getting wealthy, celebrating their demise.

Hate is growing stronger, war is in effect.

People are starting to wonder, are we free yet.

Trying hard to make a living, what's the real deal?

Tired of all the hate and killing,

That it's starting to make me ill.

We didn't ask for this, all we want is to be free.

The struggle is dismissed,

Who cares about you and me?

Everybody's killing each other,

The world's full of disgrace.

Can't seem to come together all because of self hate.

Society's making you stupid,

Make's you believe what they want.

You'll never be anything,

This is what you're being taught.

You have your own mind, you can think of yourself,

Stop acting like you're blind,

Start thinking about your health.

Don't let this life lead you, down the wrong pathway.

Think about your children, don't let them go astray.

Towards God is the straight path,

There can be only one.

Although there's other issues at hand,

We've only just begun.

You've murdered our leaders, our children too.

You've taken our teachers, to hide the truth.

What is there left, that you can do?

Fed Up

S.O.S

I watch the news,

I hear the stories.

Don't see the point,

Don't see the glory.

All I see is killin,

Why must it be?

It's got me crying so much,

That I can't see.

Stop hurting the people,

Stop bringing us down.

As I drive in my car,

I look around.

Can't stand what I'm seeing,

So I look up at the clouds.

Praying God please help,

Stop the pain and killing.

Got drugs in the streets,

And the children chasing it.

Trying to get the money and

Attention the best way they can.

Why must it be?

Why must it be?

Got me crying so much,

That I can't see.

I walk around in life,

With tears in my eyes.

I can't seem to stop crying,

It hurt so much inside.

The time.

This life.

My God.

Please help.

LIFE

-Time and the misuse of it.

-Dark Shadows drifting through the night.

-Space of which we have no more.

TIME - You only have one life to live.

-Why should one just sit around worrying all the time?

-Why be angry at the world or even yourself.

-Why sit around crying and growing old too soon.

-Have Fun! Spend time with your kids, go out on the town or have a lovely evening at home.

Why Not? You only have one life.

DARK SHADOWS - How well do you know one another?

-How well do you know yourself? Do you trust you?

-Do you believe in you? Can you depend on you?

-Knowing someone else is almost like knowing yourself.

-Everyone has them, but you have to trust someone.

Even yourself.

SPACE - The most peaceful emptiness.

16

-Is it really just emptiness?

Or is there something more?

-Is it just nothing? No I don't believe so.

-It's so amazingly quiet and beautiful.

-It's void of all the noise, anger, greed and killing.

-It's void of all the loneliness and the hurting.

Isn't it beautiful, Isn't it -------------------.

INTAKE

I'm sick and tired of going through changes

Trying to make it in this world.

I work hard every day, to earn my pay.

I deserve more.

People always trying to keep me down,

And they wonder why I wear a frown.

17

Although I haven't went to college for some years,

I know I have shed many tears.

With all the problems trying to do what's right,

In the early morning and through the dark night.

I'm not sitting on my butt collecting welfare,

I have a job, I work, and I do care.

About how my kids grow up

And the lessons they learn,

I don't need a lecture; I've already been burnt.

I love my children more than anything in this world,

That's why I am their teacher

Both my boys and my girls.

I will make sure they have the things they need,

I know I can do it if people stop dogging me.

Always knocking me down when things are going good,

They say they will help me, which is what I understood.

That's not true, they lied, and they just wanted to know,

If they could control me and how far will they could go.

I know I have a lot of anger built up inside,

Life can be a bitch, no need to ask why.

I've never been prejudice as you already know,

But, they have too much power you know how it goes.

I might go to prison for a short amount of time,

But, it might not be all bad for a little piece of mind.

It's a tough world out there some people can't take it,

But I'm a strong black woman I know I can make it.

They will not keep me down no matter how hard they try,

I'm a born survivor, I will survive.

Running

Changes in life,

Can't be denied.

Free from them you can't be

What must you do?

But flee.

From what are you running?

From who?

Why must we run?

Is it for help or fun?

Where will you go?

Can you go?

When do you think?

You can escape you?

Never.

Not even in a blink.

No matter what, who, why or when,

You will always have you in the end.

TRAPPED

I don't know what to think.

I don't think I'm better than anyone, Do I?

I don't think I'm above nor beyond anyone, Do I?

I came from that same ghetto,

Cried them same tears,

Lived that same misery.

But I got out, Did I?

Am I still trapped in that same hell?

Just moved up to a different cell.

What number am I?

How many of us are there?

I try and try. Am I wrong?

Am I to stop trying to move on?

On to a better place,

To a better time,

A better life.

Am I just trapped?

Is there a chance?

Um, a possibility?

21

Am I wrong?

Trying and trying to move on.

Where am I?

Where can I go?

Can anyone hear me?

Is there anybody out there?

Maybe I'm still trapped.

STRESSIN

Stressin, jestin, messin around,

Don't know if I'm going up or down.

Stress kills and so does pills,

You got to take the pills,

To kill the stress that makes you ill.

Headaches that life brings,

Let freedom ring,

Freedom, what is that?

Do we have, have we had, is it real?

STOP

Treading on water,

Wading in the pool.

People going shopping

Getting ready for school.

Hovering in the air,

People everywhere.

Stop the violence,

Keep the silence.

Quit the fighting,

Keep it quiet,

Everybody do their share.

Flashlight

Light that's needed in the midst of darkness,

When emergencies arise

And everything blows out.

Take the flash and light,

And everything will work out.

What do you do when it gets dark?

Fix the problem that is the start.

Lying in darkness thinking to myself,

About life's difficulties and my health.

Without light I will get hurt,

I will fall, bump my head or get burnt.

Have to get to the circuits,

Turn the lights back on.

Need a key and a flashlight,

To see which wall it's on.

Open the case, click the switch,

The lights are back on, and that is it.

No more darkness.

LAY (Focus)

As still as a hummingbird eating a flower,

Going from one to the other, hour after hour.

Not moving fast, not moving slow,

Which way do I go?

Careers, Bills, Entertainment, Life,

What's wrong? What is right?

Can you pick one? How do you know?

Which one to start with? Which way to go?

I have to move, I have to do.

Juggling this one, juggling that,

Never knowing where it's at.

Being told to slow down,

How slow can I go?

As still as a snowman,

In the midst of the snow.

Got to move, Can't stop now,

Time is running fast, Time is running out.

Not getting any younger, Time don't stand still,

25

Slow down, start with one, and take a chill pill.

Just Lay.

A thru Z

Always Be Careful.

Don't Engage Four Girls.

Have Information.

Just Keep Love Mindful.

Never Open Papers.

Quiet Roads Swiftly.

Toughen Up Very Wisely.

X-ray Your Zen.

Going

We tried to go,

But we didn't know.

The tickets were fast,

And the ride was slow.

We tried to rent,

I guess it wasn't meant.

No matter which way we turned,

The bridges were burned.

We tried and we tried,

But nothing went right.

So we did not go,

That day was a no.

We tried the next day,

Nothing got in the way.

We were spared the day before,

We had signs from the sky to the floor.

Next day we took a bus,

Nothing went wrong so that we trust.

A lot of sitting, a lot of hours,

A lot of people, a lot of crowds.

Next time we'll take the car,

It's a better way to travel by far.

Or maybe we'll take a train,

You can sleep lying down so there's no strain.

No strain in your neck,

No strain in your back.

No wondering about the time,

Or where you're at.

No wondering and thinking

You're gonna die,

When the driver goes to sleep

And swerve to the side.

CHAPTER 2

God Is Real

In this chapter I'm remembering those that are special to me that I lost as well as remembering God. On this road to happiness you must be careful what you do, say and ask for because God is with you always. You never know when it's your time so do what's right so you can assure your spot in a better place with him.

THE ROAD TO HAPPINESS

The road to happiness,

It's a lonely one you see.

Filled with ups and downs,

Smiles and frowns,

Good and bad,

Happy and sad,

A lot of life's pains and misery's.

Sometimes the road to happiness

Can include a lot of stress.

It depend on the people you deal with,

The cheating, the fighting and the bullshit.

When you're seeking happiness,

You must look in the right place.

Not bars, not clubs,

Not on the corner staring off into space.

Happiness is not going to just come to you,

It's not going to walk up and knock on the door,

Like a job you have to do the right thing

Cover up, be respectful and more.

If you act like a whore,

That's what he'll want you for.

He'll want you for ass and tits,

Not your mind, but you body that's it,

On the road to happiness.

If you act like a lady,

Not flaunt your body, but your brain.

He'll treat you respectfully,

Like the lady you acclaim to be.

Which is what you want anyway.

For him to talk to your face

Not to talk to your breast.

Like you have a face on your chest,

On the road to happiness.

Once you find happiness

You'll know its true,

It's the feeling that's inside

Between him and you.

Make sure you do your best,

On the road to happiness.

COVER

Skin is clothing to cover the soul,

Cover the blessings, cover the sin.

Cover where you begin and where you end.

Make sure you're clean; make sure you're blessed,

Take care of the books on your right and your left.

The good that you do go in the book on your right,

Which means you'll go up high to Paradise in the sky.

The bad that you do go in the book on your left,

Which means you'll go down, Hell the only place left.

Keep yourself covered it's no body's business,

Don't tell nobody nothing, leave no witnesses.

Everyone will be a witness to the deeds that you do,

So make sure you keep it between yourself and you.

Cover.

THE BRINGER

(Dedicated to Amma Faat'timah)

Amma you were the bringer of truth,

The bringer of light,

The bringer of blessings,

The bringer of my beginning.

You are an angel,

With wings that reach across the world.

You've been a bringer to many

And will always be remembered.

I pray,

That I have what it takes

To be like you,

And bring the truth.

I know I've strayed,

But my memory of you stays.

Inside of my heart,

Never letting you depart.

From my mind.

From my soul.

Deep down inside,

I'll always hold you close.

If there was ever a guardian angel,

Beside my grandmother,

You're the one I would want.

To be Allah's watcher,

To watch over me.

And make sure I'll always be,

On the straight path.

The path of the Muslims.

The path of the righteous.

The followers of the Prophets.

The path of Allah.

You were there to teach,

Not there to preach.

You extended you hands,

And made us understand.

You took your time,

Made sure we got it right.

You gave your help to everyone in need,

You reached out to me.

For that I am grateful,

And forever faithful.

And Allah knows best,

You are one of the best.

Muslims I know.

When you left,

It was your time.

To be with him,

To be by his side.

Which I know Insha-Allah you'll be

For all eternity.

I just pray I can follow your footsteps,

As you followed the Prophets.

And be among them in the time of Qiyamah.

And live among them for all eternity.

Remember

Losing a loved one is the hardest thing in the world

To put in words for a boy or a girl.

Trying to say what you feel,

Say what's in your heart,

How your body won't stop shaking,

Or how your mind won't stop wondering.

Thinking about all the good times you had

And even the bad ones.

Nothing could ever replace it,

No one could ever replace him.

Trying to put your faith in God to get you by,

But you're overrun by anger and hatred inside.

Wanting to spend the rest of your lives together,

Maybe even die together.

We make our plans in life

And God makes plans to.

God is the best of planners

He had other plans for him.

He wanted him to come home.

Remembering him and the good times

Will keep your heart strong so you can move on.

No one can ever say they know how you feel,

You didn't only lose a twin you lost your best friend.

The connection you have will always be there,

Give a toast to him on your birthday as if he was here.

Keep his memory alive; keep him in your thoughts,

Always strive to do better, try to make it to the top.

Death is a part of life we all have to go one day,

Try to live your life to the fullest and the best that you can

So when it's your turn to go home your books will be given in the

Right hand.

He is at peace; he is with god above,

Don't mourn his death, celebrate his love.

The Love he had for his family, his children and his life,

Will always live in our hearts, our souls and our minds.

And will always keep him alive.

Thinking of You

Thinking of you and the joyful times we had,

Runs in my mind like the constant drip of a leaky faucet.

Remembering the good times we had when we were younger,

Watching you all play basketball never missing a game.

Playing fireworks war on the fourth of July,

And every year having a big gathering in Washington Park.

Almost like a family and friend reunion.

We ate barbecue till we were blue in the face,

Listened to the live bands you all got to come out there,

Played softball, volleyball and just had a great time enjoying each

Others company.

It would have never been the same without you there.

Looking at you always thinking you were my father,

Until I saw your nice smile. I knew it could only be you.

I am so sorry that I didn't get to say goodbye

And that I stayed away so long.

I looked forward to seeing you this August at the parade,

Introducing you to my children and just being able to laugh

Together again.

The tears just won't stop pouring from my eyes as I think of you,

I can't believe you're gone,

But I guess God had other plans.

You will always be in my heart and in my thoughts,

Things will never be the same without you.

I Love You.

NO TURNING BACK

Tell me what you gonna do,

When God comes to you.

Tell me what you gonna feel,

When you realize it's real.

Spending your life trying to earn the world,

The world is not the big pearl.

40

The Pearl is Paradise or Heaven as you call it,

What you get in this world ain't worth a split.

A banana split or anything else,

Is that all you care about is yourself?

You can't take it with you when you die,

You can only take your deeds on your right and left side.

Think about your deeds and the things you do,

The earth begged God not to create you.

Because all you do is hurt and destroy everything,

The atmospheres, the earth, even the human beings.

Why it is? What do you want?

What? You won't be happy 'till there's none,

No one, Zilch, nothing left,

No one to murder or to lie on,

No more theft, No one to rely on.

That's it, No more, it is the end,

Which makes us no better than the Jinn.

41

Self destruction is all it was,

We destroyed earth, ourselves and the Love.

Now here's Judgment Day only two places to go,

Heaven or Hell, How will you know?

Think about your deeds and the things you did,

That lets you know where you're going in the end.

Then there's "NO TURNING BACK!!!"

Written By: Faa'timah AbdurRab

Co Writer: LaBhali Razi

CHAPTER 3

If I Only Knew

Your very first relationship is your hardest and the one that teaches you the most. "Awww, you're first Love" Then come children, cheating, arguing, loneliness, despair and then strength and it's all so that you can learn what you do and don't want.

I THOUGHT

I thought I finally found someone who loves me

As much as I love them.

I thought the love I found was truly mines.

I thought our love was strong enough to last through all times.

But now I know I just thought!

I thought I was doing what was right,

Being a mom as well as a wife.

Maybe I was wrong to think,

The love we had wasn't just a thing.

Maybe it wasn't love at all.

Why must I always take the fall?

Maybe that's what the problem is,

I just thought!

Now what must I do with all these thoughts?

Having great days, taking long walks.

Living and loving all night long,

Never wanting to answer the phone.

Now I wonder what might be clear,

Do you love me or must I fear.

That one day I'll be without you,

Holding you, hugging you, kissing you.

Maybe it wasn't love at all.

Why must I always take the fall?

Maybe that's what the problem is,

I Just Thought!

DARK SHADOWS

No one knows the dark shadows of a person.

How they feel, think or react to certain situations.

The dark shadows could be pain or loneliness.

It might even be murder.

You will never know just by meeting someone,

What they are thinking or feeling inside.

You can't just categorize everyone as being the same, because of

Their color, neighborhood or just because they end up in the same

Place in life.

Everyone has different trials and tribulations they go through,

No one deals with them the same;

No one ever feels the same.

Everyone has their own remedy for pain.

Just as everyone has their own remedy for life.

Don't ever think you know someone,

Even if you've known them for years.

Because, No one will ever reveal their entire selves to you, no

Matter whom you are, or how much they feel they know you.

You'll never understand the dark shadows of anyone.

Just as you will never understand the Dark Shadows of this world.

WHERE DO I STAND

What kind of Love you have for me,

I don't understand what it's supposed to be?

I'm loving your mind, body and soul,

But you're giving your love to someone else to take hold.

Why do you keep doing this to me?

All I want is for you to love me.

Is old girl, drugs and your boys more important?

Or does the love you have for me lie still and dormant?

Maybe there is no love at all,

Maybe your feelings for me are like the trees in the fall.

Changing colors, dying and falling to the ground,

Without life, without substance and without making a sound.

Maybe the feeling you have is just infatuation?

Or maybe it's lust, sexual frustration?

It has to be more, sex is not enough,

We should just be friends

Realize this relationship is a bust.

Where do I stand?

TRUE COLORS

Traveled half around the world to make a change,

A change in our lives.

For the better of us and the better of our children,

And still they try and knock us down from way across the world.

What more is it you have to say?

We weren't together even when you were in my face.

We weren't a family, you just pretended so you could save face,

But behind closed doors you were no more than a fucking disgrace.

I did my best to try and hold my words,

But my tongue began to sing like a mocking bird.

My body's even tired of the shit you do,

I tried to hold it back, but even my fingers say fuck you.

I gave you my trust and you stomped all over it,

I gave you my love and you poked a hole in it with a pin.

I've always been supportive of you through thick and thin,

And you stabbed me in the back in the end.

I already had no trust, no trust, no trust,

For no one else but family

But family, but family,

Man but So Called family.

I trust no one, I Trust No One,

TRUST NO ONE, BUT GOD!

IN OR OUT

We were together for a long time,

I don't know what happened.

What happened to the time?

In the beginning we were happy,

We had our ups and downs.

But, when we had children,

It changed a lot of things around.

Are you gonna be in or out of their lives,

They're our responsibility.

Both you and me,

They are not only mines.

Just because you have another love in your life,

Doesn't mean you forget the one's you brought into this world.

Whether it's a boy or a girl,

I'll always be by their side.

You can't keep coming in and out of their lives,

I'd rather you just turn and say goodbye.

"Cause I'll be there for them, and I'm gonna love them.

I'm gonna give them everything they need,

To make sure they grow up happy.

They don't need a part-time father,

You haven't been there so don't bother.

They need someone there for them,

To wash the tears away.

And bring sunshine into their day,

They get that from me their mother.

50

CHAPTER 4

The Let Down

This chapter was a hard one because at the time I was truly seriously hurting. My hurt came from all the people that was suppose to Love me. It's very easy not to trust strangers because when they hurt you, you just brush it off because it means nothing, but when it's coming from those that suppose to Love you, because you want to trust them, so when they hurt you it's very hard to swallow like a knot stuck in your throat. It's very hard to just get over.

YOU ARE

How can you talk, you selfish, hateful, bitches?

You're nothing but two-bit hoes.

You're no better than anyone else,

Everyone will soon know just who you really are.

Then you won't be able to talk about anyone else.

You picked the wrong woman's child to fuck with,

Fucking with me is one thing I can handle it.

I'll just blow you off like you mean nothing,

Because you don't,

But when you start fucking with my kids,

That's where I draw the line.

No one fucks with my kids.

You are nothing to me now,

The Gloves Are Off!

EVIL IS AS EVIL DOES

What more is there you have to say?

The ones you treated badly have gone away.

Who are you going to talk about now?

Who is there left for you to let down?

You have what you want,

Now I hope you're happy.

You have all you need,

Your one true family.

You no longer have my family,

To place your hatred upon.

Now I hope you get everything you deserve,

For the evils ones that you are.

You are a hateful people,

And you deserve to be alone.

I hope everyone leaves you alone,

In your evil infested home.

You no longer have me and my family

53

To place your evil upon,

God don't like ugly,

And I pray he deals with you one by one.

NOTHING THERE

Everything has a beginning and an end,

You just have to find out where.

Or sometimes there's just nothing, nowhere to begin,

No matter what you think is there.

Just as people believe in god, but don't see him,

Although you can't see him he is still there.

He's watching over what he created, the world,

The people, their pain and misery.

This world use to be full,

Filled with trees, grass, clear water and beauty.

Now the world is dull,

Filled with greed, pollution, heartache and misery.

What happened to all the green, the blue, the nice clear sky?

Where did all the happiness go, where and why?

We try our best to find a serene place to be,

What happened? Is there anywhere left for me?

Nothings all we have,

Nothings all that's there.

What is there left for us to share,

Nothing, There's Nothing There!

CHAPTER 5

Dreaming

This chapter is just about dreams of fantasies of different types of Love. Just showing some Love.

FORBIDDEN LOVE

I write this letter all about you to get things off my chest; I've been holding it in for so long it's been like holding my breath.

I know that you and I could never be because we both love another, but the thought of being with you for just one moment is more than I could hope for.

Your sexy eyes, your soft smooth skin makes me want to get close to you,

But if for one instant that was to happen who knows what might be. I think about you every day, how you tease and joke with me,

The only thing is I feel you know, you're only too shy to show.

Sometimes when you sit and talk to me, I watch your sexy lips. Wanting so bad to kiss you and to grab those sexy hips.

 I know you know what you're doing to me you better stop playing around, you don't know me like you think you do I have no problem with messing around.

I'll rub you, kiss you and lick you everywhere you can imagine, I'll make you forget all about your love and your marriage.

I'm a freaky person inside and out with a romantic imagination, I'll romance you, make you feel real special and fulfill your every desire.

 I know it's wrong for us to be together but curiosity has got me going, if it will make it seem better to add another person then let's get it going.

The one thing I hate about the situation is the not knowing rather

Than the knowing, I really want to tell you how I feel every time I

Get you alone.

It's so hard to read you; I don't know how you'll react and I don't

Want our friendship gone, I feel you give me signs all the time but

What if I were wrong.

What if I tried to kiss you and you slapped me, called the police and

Everything is ruined? I really want you but I can't risk, my family and

My life for a little kiss.

Should there ever come a time when you're not too shy, you'll always be welcome to kiss, touch or hug me whenever you feel the need.

I sign off my letter with a kiss, and an imagination of what could be But I understand the risk and what could happen between you and Me.

SEXUAL ROMANTIC

Sexual Romantic I do be,

Sexually aroused

From the top of my head

To the bottom of my feet.

My body long to be touched,

Held and caressed with every breath.

Breathing in and out ever so slowly,

Trying to slow the beat of my heart

And the blood from flowing

My body is so hot

The temperature of 104,

The anticipation gets heavy

As you carry me to the door.

The door opens slowly

All I can see is light,

The beautiful lights of the candles

All over from left to right.

Romance is in the air

So is the smell of sweet musk,

Can't wait to hold you baby

59

Making Love is a must.

As he lie me on the pillows

Soft and spread on the floor,

He then lit the fireplace

This warmed me even more.

I feel like this is it

We'll make love all night,

He began to feed me grapes

After he dimmed the light

After feeding me grapes

He decided to make a change,

He began slowly undressing me

Even my personal things.

As he undressed me

He began to rub me down,

Admiring every curb and essence

And slowly laying me down.

He brought out some lotion

60

CARAMEL ONIONS

So hot to the touch,

Began rubbing it all over me

Blowing and licking me with his tongue.

Ooh baby that feels so good,

Keep going don't stop

You know you do my body good.

Ooh you're driving me crazy

I can't stand it no more,

You're going to make me start screaming

People will hear me through the floor.

He licked and rubbed my body

From the top to the bottom,

Making sure he touch

Every curb, every essence, and every hole I got.

Just as I began to burst

He decided to stop,

He just don't know

If he didn't I was going to pop.

As I waited patiently

Desperately wanting him to continue,

He began to slowly undress

Saying: I just want to be in you.

Oh my God

This is what I wanted,

What I longed for,

Making Love to him

Is like getting the Big Score.

As he came to me

Kissing and caressing me,

Slowly planting himself

Where he needed to be.

As my body lunged to meet his

And we came closer together as one,

My alarm clock went off

And I woke up.

LOVE

What is Love?

Is it how a person looks that make you fall in Love?

Is it how much money is spent?

Is it the cologne that person wears that make you fall in love?

or is it the time that's shared?

Is it the look given to you from across the room that

Make you fall in love?

Is it the strut in their walk?

Is it the way they stay by your side that make you fall in love?

Is it their touch?

Is it the way they talk that make you fall in love?

Or is it when you make love?

Yes, All of the above.

Love has many meanings, but they all add up to one.

Love is many strong emotional feelings people have for each other,

Which bonds them together as one.

Love is the greatest feeling.

You could have all the Riches, Knowledge,

Power and family in the world.

It's all meaningless without love.

Think about love, the joy and happiness love has brought you.

It doesn't mean you have to have a man or woman in your life.

First you have to love yourself before you can love anyone else.

SPREAD LOVE.

CHAPTER 6

There Is Beauty In The Midst Of the Storm

This shows all the beautiful things in the world that people forget about because all the stresses in their lives. God is Great and He made it so man could enjoy the beautiful sites in the world so that when struggles seem so hard that you just can't get a handle on them, just open your eyes and look around you and remember there is beauty in the midst of the storm.

WORLD

The world has beauty, wonder and joy,

Behind all the greed, the turmoil, the ploys.

I see the blessings that God has given,

The earth, the universe and everything in it.

I know there are bad things everywhere we go,

We just have to Love and teach the good we know.

There are a lot of terrible things in this world we must endure,

If we're to live in this world peaceful,

We must remember what is pure.

What is pure in this world, God has created,

What is not, the devil is responsible

And you know he made it.

He didn't do it alone people had a hand in it,

Evil tendencies and anger in the heart and in their heads.

I have to see, the joy in me,

The joy my kids and husband has brought to me.

66

If I don't there's only pain,

That's in the brain that only drives you insane.

The world was given as a blessing,

Everything in it and around it.

Use it as it is no need for stressing,

The world can help you if you don't destroy it.

TREES

Trees are beautiful things,

Brown, green and flowing.

Sprouting and growing in the spring,

Covered in white when it's snowing.

In the summer trees are blossomed,

67

Beautiful, green and full of life.

The wonderful sight and splendor of them,

When they are alive.

In the fall the trees are dying,

Turning different colors.

Colors of red, beige and brown,

And falling from the trees.

Only to prepare itself,

For what is going to be.

In the winter the trees are dormant,

Hibernating till the next season.

Covered in the white beauty of the snow,

Till the next season when it will start to grow.

In the spring trees are it's most magnificent,

When it start to live and grow and blossom again.

I love this stage in the life of the tree,

Here you'll see the blessings of God, the powers that be.

The life of the tree,

Is like the life of everything.

Everything must live,

Everything must die.

And nothing happens without the will of God.

SKY

Clear blue sky,

Way up high.

No clouds in sight,

All through the night.

Constellation of stars,

Oh so very far.

Surrounding the moon,

Like food on a spoon.

Oh how beautiful it is.

The sun in the sky,

Like the moon is at night,

Oh what a beautiful sight.

The birds as they fly,

Like the clouds in the sky.

And the rain as it flow,

Like the storm in a window.

And the thunder claps,

Like the angry woman's slap.

As the lightning fires,

When a car flattens its tires.

Oh what a blessing it is.

RAINBOW

I look upon a rainbow,

I see here today.

It's over 90 degrees,

And hotter than I can say.

I stand here in the water,

To cool myself off.

If I don't get any cooler,

I might just pass out.

I wish upon this rainbow,

I see here today.

That the weather would cool off,

And we won't be afraid to play.

Going outside during the day,

Is just not an option.

Staying inside is much cooler,

Underneath the air condition.

A Rainbow is nice to see,

Especially a big one.

In order for that to be,

The clouds must cover the sun.

When the clouds cover the sun,

The rain starts to pour.

The world is cooled off,

The ground, the trees and much more.

Everyone loves the rain,

Although we stay inside.

Cause the thunder and lightning,

Cause some people to die.

But the rain makes a rainbow,

So big and beautiful to see.

At the end is a pot of gold,

A story told to you and me.

SUMMERTIME FUN

Waking up it's hot outside,

Sun burning your skin like fire.

Got to cool off, must get into some water,

Go to six flags, get into Hurricane Harbor.

Slides, pools and water sports,

Got to get on my swim suit and shorts.

Six Flags great America is so much fun,

Get on rides, in the water and enjoy the sun.

I like to take the kids to six flags,

But sometimes it gets boring.

So I also take them to the zoo,

Or to Botanical Gardens.

The summertime is boring when there's nothing to do,

You have to plan a lot of things for you and the kids too.

Keep the kids out of trouble,

Keep them from doing wrong.

That's all they'll do

If there's nothing going on.

Six Flags, The Zoo, Botanical Gardens,

Things the kids can do instead of causing problems.

Think About It.

THE ZOO

The zoo is a residence for animals to live,

Where people can visit and see how they live.

When I visit the zoo it sometimes makes me sad,

Because the animals look so unhappy and mad.

Sometimes they look happy or energized and such,

But I think they just do that so they'll get their lunch.

Sometimes the noise they make,

Sound as if they are crying.

Like a baby dolphin whaling,

When it's looking for its mommy.

When you look at a snake,

All he do is be lying.

Lying here, lying there,

No energy or enthusiasm anywhere.

Animals are born free,

And are meant to be predators.

That's why when you see them at the zoo,

They turn their backs to you.

They don't want to be fed their food,

They're use to catching their own.

Hunting down their prey,

And getting into the zone.

75

Right before they catch them,

And start munching on them.

Yum Yum they feel,

As they eat their prey.

They've earned the right to dine,

And they've earned the right to play.

I guess there are

Some good things about the zoo,

We learn about the different animals

And the different things they do.

There are so many different species,

They're from all over the world

For you and me to see.

I love to see the animals,

Even the insects too.

I just don't like the fact,

That they're locked up in a zoo.

You should make the zoo bigger,

More to them like a home.

Then the animals will be happier,

And seeing them will be more fun.

I can learn to love the zoo,

If the animals are happy too.

25

CHAPTER 7

My Life

"ACCEPT US FOR WHO WE ARE!"

OUR HOUSE

Our house is us; it's who we are,

Our joy, our pain, our hurt, our heart.

It's the comfort we feel in being on our own,

Everyday always coming back to our happy home.

So happy to say that this is us,

Being able to decorate, design and thus.

To be in a home of your own is great,

Now maybe we can get pass the hate.

The hate that I get from my family everyday,

Telling me that I don't know the way.

To take care of myself and my children to,

They don't know so that makes them the fool.

Making assumptions about what they think,

I really don't care, cause what they think stinks.

Our house is Love, Our house is Just.

Our house is us.

LET GO!

I thought you loved me,

But, you're always coming down on me.

I'm too old, let the string go.

I thought that you didn't want to let go,

But, now I don't think so.

Could it be jealousy?

Or maybe it's just reality.

Maybe you just realize that I'm an adult,

Old enough to take care of myself.

I can handle my own faults,

I don't need your help.

Let me go,

I am not a baby.

I have babies of my own.

Let me go,

I can take care of my responsibility,

80

I can make it on my own.

Let go, Just Let go!

Let me go, stop trying to run my life,

I don't need the arguments or the strife.

All I want is to be left alone,

In my own peaceful and happy home.

I am building a new family with my husband and children,

A life that is righteous and without sin.

Full of Love, Peace, Happiness,

Without all the pain and stress.

As you already know,

The pain and hurting has got to go.

So Just Let Go.

US

I know I am a good mother,

I do the best I can.

I'm not saying I'm the best mother,

But you will see it in the end.

In the end of a child's childhood

You will see,

The lessons they were taught

And the type of adults they grow up to be.

If you didn't teach them right

And you weren't there for them,

They will grow up disrespectful

And end up in jail.

My husband and I try to be there for ours

As well as any other child that needs it,

But unfortunately we can't save the world

The parents have to have a hand in it.

CARAMEL ONIONS

Some people dislike us for the people we are,

It really doesn't matter to us,

As long as were in good with the one above.

That's all that really matters to us.

Some people say nasty things

And talk about us for no apparent reason,

Yet they don't know us or anything about us

Maybe they're lonely or it's just the season.

I feel bad for the children that are all alone in a family full of people,

No one pays them any attention so they do what they can to get it.

Whether good or bad,

The adult don't really matter,

Because they know better

They know what they have to do.

Take care of their children

Take care of themselves

And do good till their souls are due

MIND BLOWING

Knowing how I am, been with me so long.

Why don't you understand?

Trying hard to weather the storm.

Are you a real man?

Loving me I know is a challenge,

But what good is Love without a challenge?

What good is life without a challenge?

I try to be what you want in a woman, what you want in a wife.

Am I not doing it right?

I know you say you love me for me,

But I don't love me.

I know I can't put my feelings on to you,

But what am I to do?

I try not to be angry with you I know you've done nothing wrong.

I'm just so disappointed in myself that it's portrayed wrong.

How can I love you? How can I love me?

84

How can I get back to the person in me?

I don't know its mind blowing.

Black Pearl

Should I wear black pearls?

Should I rock your world?

Life in total darkness,

Black is my color of choice.

I wear black clothes,

I wear black shoes,

Should not the pearls I wear be black to?

Is black dark and dreary?

Or is it the reality of infinity?

Infinite as the night turns to day,

As black as the beauty in your eyes.

As rich as your soul divine.

You are the black pearl

In my beautiful black world.

CHAPTER 8

My Love

Love and protect your children. They are an extension of you.

These are our babies and they are our future.

OFFSPRING

Kids are the purest, beautiful beings there could be,

Innocent of all wrongdoing if only others could see.

They are our future to soon rule the earth,

So we have to guide them from the time of birth.

Our Offspring is our babies to love.

Blessings sent from God above.

We have to show them the way.

To bring sunshine to their days.

Remember these are our babies,

Blessings sent from above.

We have to care for them,

Teach them, guide them and give them love.

They wouldn't be here if you didn't ask for them,

Now you must go make a life for them.

I see kids everyday some happy full of gleam,

Some unhappy, always frowning and mean.

No child in this world should be unhappy and sad,

No child would if you give them their childhood back.

Let them be the children they're supposed to be,

When they get older then they'll worry about responsibility.

Love begins between a child and their mother,

So stop giving them weapons of which to kill their brothers.

I don't know about our children today,

What I do know is we have to show them the way.

It's too many bad influences out here in the world,

We need more good ones to better our future,

For the next generation of boys and girls.

SEEDS

Seeds growing and blossoming into beautiful flowers.

Making their mark in the world.

That's what children are.

If you don't water them, what happens?

They die of thirst.

If you don't feed them, what happens?

They die of hunger.

If you don't love and care for them, what happens?

They die of loneliness and neglect.

And if you hurt them, what happens?

They Die!

You must Care for, Feed,

Nourish and Love your children,

So that they can blossom into beautiful flowers.

Most importantly you must

NEVER, EVER HURT THEM!

If you do, what happens?

"THEY DIE!!!"

CHAPTER 9

Beware

"PLEASE KEEP THE RAPIST AWAY FROM OUR CHILDREN!"

RAPER MAN

I'm tired of all the pedophiles

And the crazies in the world,

Going from one town to another

Kidnapping, raping and killing little girls.

What's going on in the world?

It didn't use to be this way,

Is there anywhere safe?

Safe for you and me.

I have children of my own

And I love my children dearly,

I can't imagine anyone hurting them

I can't imagine not having my babies.

I usually don't believe in the death penalty,

But now the times have changed.

I believe it will be best

If they make them suffer horribly.

Do your job get them off the street,

Because you're so call rehabilitation is dangerous for me.

You don't rehabilitate them,

You only house them momentarily.

Then when you get tired of them,

You let them loose on the world like hungry grizzlies.

If you're going to let them loose

Send them to an island of their own,

Then they can prey on each other

And leave our children alone.

CHAPTER 10

Change Is Good

Sometimes you need to move and change to do better, but you must make sure where you live is in good living condition and a good fit for your family.

MOVE OUT

Sitting here watching you,

You don't know what I'm going through.

Tried to talk to you about it once before,

I can't take it no more.

I want to move.

I want to leave.

I get down on my knees.

Lord, please help me please,

I want to move.

Tired of looking at the same faces,

I want to go, find a better place.

Ghetto fabulous people around here,

Sick and tired of what I hear.

I want to move.

Kids running from one corner to the next,

Lord, knows I've tried my best.

CARAMEL ONIONS

Not to say anything, mind my own business,

But who's going to be a witness.

When they get hurt,

I want to move.

I want to move.

I want to leave.

I get down on my knees.

Lord, please help me please,

I want to move.

Selling drugs on the corner,

Dogs and cats run the streets.

Bugs run the neighborhood,

Nothing left for you and me.

Feel like a small ant,

In this big giant world.

Trying to move where it's best,

Trying to find the big pearl.

I want to move.

Moving up, moving out,

A better place, a better route.

Can't be relaxed,

Always have to worry,

Getting down to the facts.

Trying to leave in a hurry.

I want to move.

NO RESPECT

Water bugs and mice,

You know that ain't right.

Living under the stairs, living in the walls,

Making you scared to walk down the halls.

Cockroaches and spiders,

Really making me tired.

Getting into your electronics,

Getting into your food,

Can't get a decent rest.

This shit really ain't cool.

I can't continue to live like this,

There is no comfort or enjoyment in it.

We deserve to get more respect,

We deserve to live our best.

Not living like pigs,

Living in the den.

Ghetto fabulous,

All in the hood.

This is not where I choose to live,

The landlord knows he needs to fix it.

I get no respect.

About me

I spend my life as a Mom, Wife and Homemaker.

As a homemaker I spend most of my time with my children and my husband and taking care of home and during my free time that's when I write my Poetry. I don't just stop my writing at Poetry; I've also been working on a few books of which you will get to read later. Because of my love for children I've also been working on some children stories as well.

What I've written here is different poems which show the sour and sweetness of people, the world, everything. I feel that life is like a Caramel Onion because you never know what you're going to get.

There is the nice, sweet kind, easy part of it or the mean bitter struggle that life can be

www.ingramcontent.com/pod-product-compliance
Lightning Source LLC
Chambersburg PA
CBHW032144040426
42449CB00005B/398